石林
SHI LIN XIA

畅游石林峡

The Rock Wonderland —Gorge Shilin

by Chai Fushan

柴福善 著

中国旅游出版社

Sincerely welcome friends from all over the world to visit Gorge Shilin and enjoy its natural landscape of clear air and water.

——— **An Man**

诚挚欢迎天下朋友
来石林峡 享受山
明水净的大自然

安满

柴福善

1956 年 12 月生，北京市平谷区人。曾任县委党史办副主任、县文化文物局副局长、区文化委员会副主任、区文联副主席、区政协常委、学习与文史委员会主任，现为中国作家协会会员、北京作家协会理事。

1982 年起发表文学作品，在全国多家报刊发表诗歌百余首、散文 400 余篇，多篇作品被转载，并收入多种文集。散文集《江山有待》荣获全国第五届冰心散文奖，《两栖集——柴福善散文精粹》被中国散文学会指定为 2012 年特别推荐书籍。

出版散文集《逍遥人生》《岁月无痕》《往事与乡情》《核桃树下的王蒙》《秦时明月》《江山有待》《两栖集》及校注《李锴诗文集》《我与中学生谈写作》，与古建专家罗哲文合著《中华名寺大观》《中华名塔大观》《中华名桥大观》《中华名园大观》《中华名楼大观》及《中国的世界遗产》，编著《平谷寺庙志略》《平谷古树名木图志》《志书补遗》《明代平谷志料辑校》《平谷史话（修订本）》《峪口史话》《独乐河史话》《马昌营史话》《镇罗营史话》《大兴庄史话》《刘家店史话》《东高村史话》《丫髻山》《丫髻山楹联匾额》《丫髻山碑刻》《丫髻山传说》及《丫髻山历史文化读本》，主编《泃水长歌》（三卷）《平谷文物志》等。

Chai Fushan

Born in Dec 1956, in Pinggu District, Beijing. He used to be the Deputy Director of the Party History Office of the County Party Committee, Deputy Director of the County Bureau of Culture and Cultural Relics, Deputy Director of the District Cultural Committee, Vice Chairman of the District Federation of Literary and Art Circles, a member of the District Standing Committee of the People's Political Consultative Conference, Director of the District Committee of Learning, Culture and History, currently a member of the China Writers Association and director of the Beijing Writers Association.

Since 1982, Chai Fushan has published more than 100 poems and 400 pieces of essay in domestic newspapers and magazines, and lots of them were picked and included in many anthologies. His collected works of prose *The Rivers and Mountains Await* won the Fifth National Bingxin Prose Award, and *The Collected Works of Amphibians——The Prose Essence of Chai Fushan* was specially recommended by the Chinese Prose Association to the public in 2012.

He has published prose collections including *Leisure and Carefree Life*, *Untraceable Years*, *The Past and the Affection for My Hometown*, *Wang Meng Under the Walnut Tree*, *The Bright Moon in Qin Times*, *The Rivers and Mountains Await*, *The Collected Works of Amphibians*; annotated *The Collected Works of Li Kai's Poems*, *Talking to the Middle School Students About Writing*; co-authored with ancient architecture specialist Luo Zhewen *The Grand Sight of Chinese Temples*, *The Grand Sight of Chinese Towers*, *The Grand Sight of Chinese Bridges*, *The Grand Sight of Chinese Gardens*, *The Grand Sight of Chinese Buildings and The World Cultural Relics in China*; edited *The Brief History of the Temples in Pinggu*, *The Illustrated History of the Ancient Trees in Pinggu*, *Supplements to the History Book*, *The Edition and Revision of Pinggu's History in Ming History*, *A Narrative History of Pinggu (Revised Edition)*, *A Narrative History of Yukou*, *A Narrative History of Dule River*, *A Narrative History of Machangying*, *A Narrative History of Zhenluoying*, *A Narrative History of Daxingzhuang*, *A Narrative History of Liujiadian*, *A Narrative History of Donggaocun*, *The Yaji Mountain*, *The Antithetical Couplets and the Horizontal Inscribed Boards of Yaji Mountain*, *The Tablet Inscriptions of Yaji Mountain*, *The Legends of Yaji Mountain*, and *Insights into the History and Culture of Yaji Mountain*; chiefly edited the third volume of *Intoning poems of Jushui*, *The Cultural Relics in Pinggu* and so on.

卷首语

一篇好的山水游记，本身就是一道美丽的风景。没想柴福善老师不经意做了一件对石林峡发展很有深远意义的事情，以艺术之笔，把自然山水与人文精神相融合，混沌一体，赋予了石林峡历史之韵、文化之气、山水之魂，提高景区品质的同时，更让石林峡人多年之汗水在精神层面开了花，结了果。地因文名，从此，这峡谷就更加面目清晰、精神抖擞了。

小军记于 2020 年 6 月 11 日

Preface

Vivid travel notes have scenery in themselves. This is something of far-reaching significance that Mr. Chai Fushan has done for the development of Gorge Shilin Scenic Zone. In his introduction on the history and culture of Gorge Shilin, we could learn that its natural landscape and humanistic value have merged into a unity. People who were born and live here from generation to generation devote themselves to make it greater and their efforts have turned into spiritual values which wins the well-known name for Gorge Shilin.

by Xiaojun,

June 11, 2020

石林峡景区游览路线图

The Route Map of Gorge Shilin Scenic Zone

石林峡，位于京东平谷东北部，属于燕山余脉。

石林峡景区，以自然山水为主，也有亭、桥、栈道、摩崖石刻等。如果从园林角度看，我国园林一般分为皇家王府园林、宅第园林、寺观园林、山水胜景园林等，那么石林峡无疑是一座山水胜景园林了。

Gorge Shilin, geographically belonging to the Yanshan Mountains, is located in the northeast of Pinggu District, eastern Beijing, China.

From the perspective of gardening, Chinese gardens are generally divided into four types, such as royal palace garden, mansion garden, temple garden and natural landscape garden. Accordingly, the mountainous Gorge Shilin is undoubtedly a natural landscape garden; moreover, pavilions, bridges, trestle roads and cliff stone carvings can all be seen here.

石林峡景区前迎宾桥桥头

The front end of the Yingbin Bridge in Gorge Shilin Scenic Zone

走上这座迎宾桥。

说到桥，我国古代有索桥、浮桥、梁桥和拱桥四大基本类型。索桥，一种以绳索或铁索建造的桥梁，多建于沟深水急的峡谷中。浮桥，一种以船、筏及木板为桥身而建造的桥梁。梁桥，又称平桥，一种以桥墩和横梁建造的桥梁。拱桥，与梁桥相对而言，是一种以拱券建造的桥梁。

迎宾桥，一座 5 孔石拱桥，横跨于石林河上，桥两边护以石栏。而桥头以花木搭架成一道彩虹，热情迎接天下游人。

Here comes the Yingbin Bridge. “Yingbin”, in Chinese phonetic alphabet, means welcoming visitors.

Cable bridge, floating bridge, beam bridge and arch bridge are four basic types of bridges in ancient China. A cable bridge is usually built with ropes and iron chains in steep gullies with turbulent water. Boat, raft or plank can be used as the main body of a floating bridge. A beam bridge, also known as flat bridge, shows the combination of piers and beams. In contrast to it, an arch bridge is built in a structure with a curved top that is supported by straight sides.

The Yingbin Bridge is a 5-hole stone arch bridge spanning the Shilin River with stone balusters on both sides. Decorated with flowers and plants, the rainbow-shape bridge is always the first here to welcome the visitors from all over the world.

石林峡景区前迎宾桥

The Yingbin Bridge in Gorge Shilin Scenic Zone

书法家苏适题写的“石林峡”三个大字，被作为了石林峡标

The three Chinese characters " 石林峡 " written by a Chinese calligrapher as the logo of the scenic zone

景区大门，上书“石林峡”三个大字，书写者为苏适。

当然，此苏适非彼苏轼，与宋代大文豪、书法号称苏黄米蔡四家之首的四川眉山苏轼苏东坡无关，苏适的“适”是适合的适，他是我国当代书法家。

The three Chinese characters at the entrance gate of the scenic zone, “ 石林峡 ” which means Gorge Shilin, were written by Su Shi, a Chinese contemporary calligrapher.

By the way, there were four literary masters and calligraphers in the Chinese Song Dynasty: Su Shi, Huang Tingjian, Mi Fu and Cai Xiang. They were generally called for short by their family names Su Huang Mi Cai. Among them, Su Shi was the most well-known one. But, of course, he is not the one who writes “ 石林峡 ” for the scenic zone nowadays. The names of these two calligraphers pronounce the same but are written by different Chinese characters.

石林峡

平时旅游，一到洞庭湖，就会想到洞庭天下水；到了岳阳，就会想到岳阳天下楼。那么到了京东，我自然会想到石林峡了。

人常说，五岳归来不看山，黄山归来不看岳，这是三山五岳。对于石林峡呢，我十几年前来过，前不久再来，还是想看的，并写了一篇游记散文《再访石林峡》，刊登在了《人民日报》上。

In China, Dongting Lake which is in northern Hunan Province has the most impressive scenery of its kind, and the city Yueyang gains reputation for having the greatest traditional buildings in China. Then, Gorge Shilin, I believe, should be the landmark of eastern Beijing.

We Chinese often say that perhaps you don't even bother to have a glance at any other mountain after your return from Mount Huang in Anhui province, because you have already seen the best there, but Gorge Shilin still surprises me even ten years after my first tour here. About this, I wrote a piece of travel note *To Be There in Gorge Shilin One More Time* which was then published in *People's Daily*.

湖南岳阳市岳阳楼（上图）
Yueyang Tower in Yueyang City, Hunan Province（the picture above）

泰山（下图）
Mount Tai（the picture below）

石林峡
Gorge Shilin

石林峡内小桥流水

Water flowing through a small "bridge" in Gorge Shilin

走进石林峡，看什么呢？四时不同，比如春天繁花的灿烂，夏天树木的葱绿，秋天霜叶的醉意，冬天雪花的洁白，点染得石林峡景色亦不尽相同。但主要景观是不变的，这就是：石林峡的山，石林峡的石，石林峡的水。当然也看横陈的小桥、点缀的亭子以及山顶钛合金飞碟玻璃观景台、山下金娃娃等，自然山水与人文景观构成这座山水胜景园林。

The mountains, stone and water here seemingly remain the same year after year, but Gorge Shilin never stops changing in accordance with the law of nature: the unstoppable vitality in spring, the healing green color of summer, the enchanting frozen red leaves by autumn and the snow-capped wonderland in winter. And there are more to explore, such as those man-made bridges, pavilions, the glass sightseeing platform on the top and the handicrafts that are made of solid gold. The natural and humanistic landscape here combine well.

石林峡沟谷中的滚滚巨石

The boulders in the valley of Gorge Shilin

石林峡的沉积岩（一）

The sedimentary rocks in Gorge Shilin (1)

这是一道天然峡谷，在燕山隆起的刹那形成，到今天，应该亿万年不止了。从这山峰山岩、地层地貌，能够看出远古的一片茫茫大海，如何渐渐隆起成莽莽燕山。

The natural canyon was spontaneously and gradually formed during the billions of years' geological movements under the Yanshan Mountains. Observing its rising and falling terrain and layered surface will help you learn the formation of it, turning from an endless sea in ancient time into the magnificent Yanshan Mountains nowadays.

石林峡的沉积岩（二）

The sedimentary rocks in Gorge Shilin (2)

走进峡谷，眺望峡谷两侧，山对称着高耸，这边的凸出处，恰是那边的凹陷处，大致吻合。尽管有的地方可能很窄，但也不会随意吻合在一起，除非再一次沧海桑田。两侧对峙的悬崖峭壁，宛若刀削斧斫，遮天蔽日。

Gazing into the distance, it's not hard to notice the symmetrical mountains on both sides, and sometimes the protrusions on this side roughly match the depressions on the other side. Though somewhere of the mountains look narrow and very close to each other, they won't combine into one, unless God wish to. The towering cliffs on both sides which are seemingly shaped by machete and axe almost shut out sunlight.

石林峡谷两壁对称着

The symmetrical cliffs in Gorge Shilin

石林峡巨石劈裂，仍对称着不愿分离

A boulder split in the middle still be complete

那峭壁因风雨蚕食，竟形如林状，故东侧山称东石林山，西侧山称西石林山，景区也自此得名。

The cliffs here erosed by wind and rainfall look like a “forest” made of giant and sheer rocks, and that’s how Gorge Shilin got its name. The mountains on the east are generally called The East Shilin Mountain, and the other side The West Shilin Mountain.

石林峡石林山

The Shilin Mountain in Gorge Shilin

细看石林间，一团团不凋的绿色，是石缝里顽强生存的松柏，虽不盎然也不蓬勃，却为石林点染出生机。应该是山多高水多高，不然很难孕育任何生命，包括松柏。看山岩间的崖柏，即使不是很粗，也应该不止三五十年，柏树生长极其缓慢，何况又长在缺水少土的岩缝里。

Look consciously. Among the crevices in the rocks survive the growing pines. They may not look very vigorous, but their tenacity brings vitality to the scenic zone. The water under the mountain surface must be reserved very high, or there won't be any chance to grow life here, even for cliff cypress. Look at them, seizing any chance in the crevices even without enough water or rich soil. They grow extremely slowly and probably have been here for several decades, though their trunks and branches do not look very strong.

石林峡谷峭壁上的崖柏

The cypress trees growing in the cliff crevices in Gorge Shilin

石林峭壁间松柏生长其间

The cypress trees growing out of the rock crevices in Gorge Shilin

前面一片柿子树，一些树老得都有空洞了，甚至长出了树瘤。人老生斑，树老生瘤，人树一理。

柿树原产于我国，是一种高大的落叶乔木。

平谷地区柿子树很多，主要有两种：一种结的是大柿子，称大盖儿柿；一种结的是小柿子，称小火儿柿。柿子秋后摘了是涩的，春节以后再吃，尤其带着冰碴儿吃，心底甭提多痛快了，以致形成一句俗语：瞅你，心里就像吃了大凉柿子似的。大意是说人遇事时没往心里去。当然，刚摘下的柿子也可以人工去涩，乡下称为“懒柿子”。不过，近年引进了一种甜柿子，摘下树即可食用。

由于柿与事谐音，人们就将柿子与事事如意相联系，画家也往往喜欢随手画几个柿子，悬挂厅堂。所以，人们便把这里称为“柿柿如意苑”。

There are persimmon trees over there. Some have got empty inside and even grown nodules. Trees getting nodules is like people showing spots on faces.

Originated from China, persimmon tree is a kind of tall and deciduous plant.

柿树

Persimmon trees

小火儿

Xiaohuoer Persimmor

Persimmons in Pinggu District can be roughly divided into two kinds according to fruit size: the bigger kind, "Dagaier", which means "big cap", and the smaller kind "xiaohuoer" which looks like "sparks". Persimmons picked right after autumn taste astringent. People usually put them aside and eat them after the Chinese traditional Spring Festival. Frozen persimmons, especially with ice flake on them, taste so amazing! People usually describe a person who lets a bad thing go and doesn't keep dewlling on it as he "looks like he ate an icy persimmon just now and felt so good". The astringent taste of freshly picked persimmons can be artificially removed; however, it won't bothered you anymore, because a new variety which taste very clean has been introduced.

The Chinese characters of "persimmon" and "thing" pronounce the same, so people usually use the image of persimmon to express that everything is as you wish. Paintings of several persimmons leisurely drew by painters got hung in the hall there, so people call this spot as Shishi Ruyi Park. Ruyi in Chinese means "as you wish".

大盖儿柿

Dagaier Persimmons

柿柿如意苑

Shishi Ruyi Park

在石林峡，可以仰则观象于天，俯则观法于地。
如果前行呢，就观石林峡山水了。而沿峡谷行走，真感觉天地有大美而不言，只能静静地欣赏。

Here in Gorge Shilin, you can look up to observe the astronomical phenomena, and look down to learn the law of the ground. Go ahead and then you will find that the true beauty never boasts, and the only thing you can do is to silently appreciate it .

幽深葱茏的石林峡谷

The deep and verdant Gorge Shilin

峡谷间，那些崩落的巨石，为千年万年自然所风化，更有被地震所震塌的。清康熙十八年（1779 年）旧历七月二十八，平谷地区曾发生一次八级左右的大地震。1976 年 7 月 28 日发生的唐山大地震，也波及至此。一些风化的山岩，甚至小半座山，都被震落了。说到底，这些大大小小的石头，原本就是大山的分化，填充着空旷的峡谷，成为我观览的景物。

The boulders, some of which collapsed during earthquakes, have been naturally weathered and eroded for thousands of years. On July 28 on the lunar calendar, 1779, the 18th year of the reign of the Qing Emperor Kangxi, an earthquake of magnitude 8.0 happened in Pinggu District; Tangshan Earthquake, on July 28, 1976, affected Pinggu District as well. Some weathered rocks and even half of a mountain were shaken off. These rocks and boulders are all parts of a mountain originally, and now become unique scenery here for visitors to explore.

巨石是大山的分化

Boulders that used to be
the parts of a mountain

孔子说，仁者乐山，智者乐水。身在石林峡，既可做仁者，又可做智者，只管尽情游览石林峡山水了。水在山石间流淌，清澈见底。溪水因山成曲折，山路随地作低平。我在溪边的山路上悠游地走着，感受着溪水逝者如斯、不舍昼夜地流淌。

Confucius said, “The wise find pleasure in water, the virtuous find pleasure in hills.” The scenery of mountain and water in Gorge Shilin is for all. Water flows even through the cracks and crevices, and the river bottom can be clearly seen. The creeks snake their ways along the mountain, and the paths follow the rolling ground. I took a leisure walk, accompanied by the streams flowing day and night without an end.

水在山石间流淌

Water flowing through rocks

前面有一棵杏树，一直生长在这里，为保护杏树，路为之避让了。这棵杏树确实老了，我记得前几年来时，它已长了些虫洞，但终归还是开了不少花，结了不少杏的。《人民日报》美编、画家罗雪村先生来写生，还为此欣然作了一张速写的。谁知今日再来，竟已枯死了。树其实也有寿命，据山里人说，一般杏树大概六七十年光景，到时候就慢慢老去。即使枯死了，也依然立在这里，这就是令人敬畏的生命。

而杏字与幸福、幸运的幸字谐音，故人们给这里起名为“一路有幸”，寄寓着一种美好希望与祝福。当然，古人也有一句非常著名的诗句：“春色满园关不住，一枝红杏出墙来”。在品读优美诗句的同时，对“红杏出墙”也有了另外的理解。

The apricot tree ahead has been there for years. People purposely avoided the tree when building a path. I saw it several years ago and remembered some wormholes on it; however, it unexpectedly managed to blossom and bear fruits. Mr. Luo Xuecun, an editor of *People's Daily* and painter, once made a sketch for it. How could we believe it withered today. Plants have their lifetimes. For apricot trees, it should be about 60 to 70 years on average. Apricot trees grow old slowly and then die as human do, but they remain firm and erect after death. We must pay awe to life!

The Chinese character of “Apricot” is a homonym of that of “luck”, so people name this road making use of the same pronunciation. It literally means “all the way down with apricots”; moreover, it contains good wish as “all the way down with good luck”. There is a traditional Chinese poem writing as “The spring scenery within the garden could never be enclosed, and a branch of apricot tree has stretched outside the wall”. People usually compare a wife of great charm as “a red apricot”. When you mention to a man that his “red apricot” is growing to the outside, you mean his wife is having an affair with another man.

一路有幸

All the way down with good luck

峡谷越来越深了，高峰入云，两侧石壁，上负危岩，下临深谷。诸峰排列，姿态各异。怪石嶙峋，崔嵬峥嵘。鬼斧神工，诗情画意。宏大气势，挺拔壮观。直引得画家、摄影家、诗人、作家，争相前来写生创作。

As you can see, the gorge is going deeper and deeper. The peaks of both sides are arranged in various poses and hidden in the clouds. Stretching out to the sky and setting roots to the ground, the towering but rugged cliffs look poetically spectacular and must be created by heaven. Here is totally a paradise for painters, photographers, poets and writers.

2015 年 6 月，人民日报罗雪村先生在石林峡写生

Mr. Luo Xuecun of *People's Daily* making sketches in Gorge Shilin in June 2015

石林峡危岩巨石

Crags in Gorge Shilin

石林峡山水相依

The interdependent water and mountain in Gorge Shilin

峡谷壁立，山泉涌流。山以水为血脉，以烟云为神采。可以说，山得水而活，也就是山有了水，就充满了灵动，不然就呆板了；水得山而媚，水有了山，就焕发出魅力，不然就平淡了。

Cliffs here stand uprightly, and springs surge. Water gives mountain vitality, as what vessels do for a body. A mountain becomes lively with water, or it will be dull and boring, and vise versa.

石林峡山水相依

The interdependent water
and mountain in Gorge Shilin

有山有水，水在峡谷间流动，就会聚而成潭。石林峡号称九瀑十八潭，是说石林峡潭多、瀑多。前面这山崖，每到雨季，山上涵养的水就会从山崖缝中流泄下来，落入潭中，故名崖泻天浆。

The flowing water here gathers into pools. Peoples say Gorge Shilin possesses "nine waterfalls and eighteen pools", which means the large number of waterfalls and pools here. In rainy season, water conserved above rushes out of cliff convices and falls down into the pools. It is vividly called "Ya Xie Tian Jiang", which means the water from heaven spilling out of the cliff.

崖泻天浆

The water from heaven rushing out of the cliff

面对不同的山石崖壁，总要起个适当的名字，以便人们欣赏。每走到前面崖壁之下，尤其在炎炎夏日，就颇觉凉爽，故称清凉小世界。而在山石的缝隙间，游人往往随手竖着倚放一根根小木棍，或有吉祥、顺畅、安康的冀望之意吧。

Facing rocks and cliffs in different shapes, we never get bored to name every beauty spot we meet here. An appropriate name can do lots of help. Here is an example. The cliff in front making there cooler than other places, especially in summer, so the spot is called The Little Cool World. Tourists put wooden sticks between the gap of layered rocks leaning against the cliff to pray for auspiciousness, smooth life and good health.

清凉小世界

The Little Cool World

山石间游人随手竖着倚放一根根小木棍，以冀望吉祥、顺畅、安康

Visitors put wooden sticks between the gap of layered rocks leaning against the cliff to pray for auspiciousness, smooth life and good health

平谷金海石“燕山魂”（刘守东收藏）

Jinhai Stone, "The Soul of Yanshan Mountains", collected by Liu Shoudong

幽幽峡谷里，散落的这些石头上，有着或繁复、或简约、或富丽、或质朴的纹饰，你或许真以为是哪位大画家的手笔，其实是自然与时光的描摹与沧桑。平谷有种奇石——金海石，就是石面以纹饰取胜，石林峡里，随处可见这些大大小小的金海石呢。

Simple or complicated, superb or rustic, naturally formed patterns and grains of different kinds can been clearly seen on these scattered stones. You may consider them the handwritings left by artists. That is actually what has been left after God of nature and God of time had finished up their talks. Regionally, Pinggu District has a peculiar kind of stone, called Jinhai stone, which in small or large size can be seen here.

石林峡沟谷中巨石石面图画

A piece of "painting" on a boulder's surface in Gorge Shilin

京东第一石，极言其体积庞大，当有两间房子大小，说巨石名副其实。

The largest boulder in eastern Beijing looks as large as two ordinary rooms of an apartment and it is indeed worthy of the name.

京东第一石

The largest boulder in eastern Beijing

飞来石，北侧崖壁上，一石千年万年摇摇欲坠而不坠。真不知从哪里来的，莫非天外飞来之物么？

On the north side of the cliff is a boulder that looks shaky and unsteady, but it never rolls down during the last thousands of years. No one could tell where it came from. Maybe from heaven.

飞来石

The boulder from heaven

背石

Carry the boulder on your back

这倾斜的巨石，背（bèi）身石下，正可一背（bēi）。摆个背好姿势照相可以，真背，不止三五万斤，没谁能背动，除非具有洪荒之力。再者，真有人能背动，恐怕早背走了，也就没了这一景。

Bend with your back to the tilted boulder and pretend to carry it on your back. Then, cheese! However, this pose is just for taking pictures. Nobody is able to move a boulder of ten more tons except Samson in Holy Bible; however, Samson never did this before, or there won't be any chance for us to see it today.

一方大石，从山上滚落时恰被一树随意一抵，石借惯势下倾，树依定力上挺，瞬间倾挺为一种平衡，一下就平衡为绝妙风景。而这树是桑树，谁知结的是紫桑葚还是白桑葚？其实，这棵桑树奇就奇在一直没结过桑葚，难道桑树也有雌雄？不得而知。

Another giant rock rolled down under the law of gravity and got stuck by a tree growing upward. What a miracle! At a moment they got perfectly balanced and now become a fabulous tourist spot. It’s so strange that the mulberry tree never grows any fruit and no one knows for sure the color of it, purple or white. Has mulberry tree a gender? Is it the reason why it grows no fruit?

一木千钧

The perfect balance between a giant rock and a tree

小桥
A beam bridge with iron frame in Gorge Shilin

走上这座小桥，铁架上铺横木。在其他地方，我也走过两头有桥墩、上面铺着大条石的石桥，这类桥被称为平桥或梁桥，为我国古桥的重要类型之一。

The bridge here is paved with planks on its iron frame. This kind of bridge with piers at both sides and large planks or bricks laying on the surface is usually called beam bridge, or flat bridge, which is a typical type of the traditional Chinese bridges. I saw and walked through this kind of bridge somewhere else before.

石林峡断石

A huge rock neatly split into two halves

小桥边一巨石，中间齐茬茬断作两截，应是天力所断，而非人力所为。断裂的石缝窄窄的，以前桥在旁边，就有人至此穿来穿去，以此为趣。我不敢贸然去穿，担心两半石一时心血来潮合并一起，躲闪不及，再想出来大概要等地老天荒了。

A huge rock near the bridge cracks neatly in the middle and breaks into two by natural power. People who visit here usually enjoy the fun of walking through the narrow gap between them, but I won't try, in case the two halves have their plan to merge and get me stuck there. If so, I can not wait that long, maybe thousands of years, for them to split again and set me free.

左侧这块大石上，坐一姑娘塑像。姑娘叫霞姑，不知是旧传，还是新编，大致是说霞姑与青梅竹马的樵夫三郎相爱，外族入侵，三郎应征从军，久未归来，霞姑就每天坐大石上盼望。久而久之，她化作了一尊塑像，这石便称霞姑石了。

On the left boulder is the statue of a girl, Xia Gu. It's generally said that Xia Gu's childhood sweetheart San Lang, a woodcutter, joined in the army to resist foreign invaders and he never returned. Having been there and waiting for her lover day after day, Xia Gu finally turned into a statue. This may be an old legend or a new-edited story. No one knows for sure.

霞姑石

The statue of Xia Gu

左侧有个天然洞穴，名罗汉洞，洞内塑有伏虎罗汉。佛教约东汉初年传入我国，佛祖、菩萨，下面就是罗汉了。常见的在大雄宝殿佛祖释迦牟尼两侧，有十六罗汉或十八罗汉。实际上，唐以前是十六罗汉，唐以后才增加到十八罗汉。当然，一些庙宇中也有如五百罗汉，就需另建殿堂了，如北京碧云寺就有罗汉堂。

There is a natural cave on the left called The Luohan Cave (The Arhat Cave) with a statue of Fuhu Arhat (Tiger Taming Arhat) in it. Buddhism was firstly introduced to China in the early years of Eastern Han Dynasty; then, people gradually became familiar to Buddha, Bodhisattva and arhat. The Sixteen Arhats or the Eighteen Arhats are commonly seen sitting symmetrically on the both sides of Buddha Shakyamuni in the Great Buddha's Hall. There were 16 arhats originally, and increased to 18 after Tang Dynasty. Some temples have special halls for arhats, such as the Arhat Hall for its Five-Hundred Arhats in Biyun Temple, Beijing.

北京碧云寺罗汉堂中罗汉像

The arhat images in the Arhat Hall in Biyun Temple, Beijing

罗汉洞

The Luohan Cave (The Arhat Cave)

通往罗汉洞的既窄且浅的溪流中，垫着两三块石头，我们可以踏着过去。其实，这也是一种简陋的石梁桥，又称“踏步桥”或“跳墩子”。我们的祖先，面对一道不深也不甚宽的河流，迈一步又迈不过去，会就地随手寻找三两块儿石头一垫，或找根木头横着两岸一搭，登踏着就过去了。这些踏墩子或独木桥，就是人类创造的最原始的桥梁。

In the narrow and shallow stream leading to the Arhat Cave, stones are casually arranged across the stream for people to tread. Those simply placed rocks function as a beam bridge which is called The Stepping Bridge or The Jumping Piers here. Taking one step could not help you cross a stream or a river which is neither that deep nor wide, but two or three rocks arranged in line or a piece of crossing wood will make it easier. Stone piers and single-wood bridge are the most primitive man-made bridges.

踏步桥

The Stepping Bridge (The Jumping Piers)

石林峡谷一路溪水不绝，时缓时急，时宽时窄，宽阔处一踅，便聚而为潭。溪水奔腾着，跳跃着，滋润着整个峡谷，使峡谷葱茏，充满着诗意。不仅水皆缥碧，游鱼细石，直视无碍，而且细听夏日里蝉鸣鸟语，蝉则千啭不穷，鸟则百叫无绝。放开眼，更有千岩竞秀，百壑争流，草木蒙笼其上，若云兴霞蔚，置身其间，使人应接不暇。

Endless streams meander slowly or urgently forward along the gorge, become narrow or wide sometimes and gather into pools in wide areas. Nourishing the whole gorge, water brings vitality and sense of pure poetry here. Streams look transparent and the scene of fish playing hide-and-seek among the rocks can be clearly seen. Listen! Cicadas shrill and birds twitter. Look around! You will be overwhelmed by the water, trees and clouds that contend with each other to show thair charm.

石林峡的潭水（一）

A natural water pool in Gorge Shilin (1)

石林峡的潭水（二）

A natural water pool in Gorge Shilin (2)

再往前走，就是石林峡谷最为曲折、狭窄的地方了，峡谷两侧最窄处仅两三米，尤其右侧崖棚，较为低矮，且探了出来，大家观赏景色的同时，一定注意上面，不要碰头。

Keep going ahead. Here we are at the most tortuous and narrowest site in the gorge which is only two to three meters wide. Especially, the rocks on your right stretching out above your head are relatively low. People need to watch out not to hurt their heads when looking at the distant spotlights.

回头再看石林峡狭窄处

Looking back at the most tortuous and narrowest site in Gorge Shilin

石林峡狭窄处

The most tortuous and narrowest site in Gorge Shilin

逆水而上，时时见到一些小的瀑流。右侧崖壁，上下一道山凹，着满黑魆魆水的痕迹。雨季来临，这里就瀑布腾泄了。旧称“天蛙台”，即是此景。

Go against the stream and you can see the small waterfalls sometimes and somewhere. The dark traces on the cliff surface that have been gradually left by flowing water look slightly concave. In rainy seasons, there will be a waterfall rushing out through the cliff. The spotlight is called “Tian Wa Tai”, the Platform of Celestial Frog.

崖壁被流水冲出的一道山凹

The concave traces on the cliff surface left by flowing water

天蛙台瀑布

The waterfall near the Platform of Celestial Frog

当至峡谷绝壁处，一道瀑布轰鸣着飞泻而下，这便是石林瀑布了。

Go deep inside the gorge to the end with sheer precipices, and you will see the Shilin Waterfall roaring down.

石林飞瀑

The Shilin Waterfall in Gorge Shilin

转身，沿着另一侧山路回走，就到了天梯。

天梯，足有 200 余级阶梯，且很陡峭，上天能是件容易的事吗？到这里石林峡已行程大半，大家是否有些累了呢？要走上这陡峭的 200 级阶梯，是需要些体力与脚力的。

行百里者半九十，成功就在最后的坚持与努力之中！不过，累了可以歇歇再登。

而登上天梯，就意味着到了天界，可以看到下面看不到的绝妙景观，这就是气势磅礴的九天飞瀑。

Turn around and go back along the path on the other side. There will be “Tian Ti”, The Ladder to Heaven.

The Ladder to Heaven has more than 200 stairs. How could it be easy to reach heaven? Here you have been halfway in Gorge Shilin. To climb the 200-stair ladder demands strong legs and enough energy.

Sustain your effort especially when your goal is nearly achieved, because people who have embarked on a one-hundred-mile journey may fall by the way side. But it’s all right to have a rest before you continue.

Every step on the ladder makes you one bit closer to the sky! From there, you will see by your own eyes the fabulous landscape that you can never imagine below. There will be the magnificent Jiutian Waterfall (The Waterfall from the Highest of Heavens).

天梯（一）

The Ladder to Heaven (1)

天梯（二）

The Ladder to Heaven (2)

一只蝴蝶与一片枯叶

A butterfly and a piece of dead leaf

走在天路上，飞瀑就在前面。

峡谷游览，我想到一段禅语：见山是山，见水是水；而后，见山不是山，见水不是水；最终，见山还是山，见水还是水。这是禅的三重境界，石林峡我不止一次来，似乎说不清见的是山还是水了。

一只蝴蝶，翩翩地落下了。落在一片枯叶前，是把枯叶当作同类了么？

Walking along this way will get you to the waterfall right there.

The trip here reminds me of the progressive levels of the realization of truth in Zen Buddhism: the fool, the vulgar and the wise see different things when they are facing the same things. I have visited Gorge Shilin several times and it can always bring me something new.

A butterfly gracefully settled near a piece of dead leaf. It probably mistook the dead leaf for a friend of its kind.

通往九天飞瀑的天路

The path to The Jiutian Waterfall

行到水穷处，坐看云起时。前面已是溪水尽头，尽头是峡谷绝壁。可峡谷绝壁不是峡谷绝笔，而是一道绝胜风景。但见山顶一瀑水流，冲出一凹缺口，急遽地从天而降，直挂黑黝黝绝壁，犹如一条白练。壁上山石突兀，白练被分割为几缕，眨眼间就飞落壁底了，这就是石林峡奇观九天飞瀑。

常言年深日久，水滴石穿，这里不止石穿了，飞瀑竟把壁底冲成一巨大石潭！飞瀑成潭，多少年来一直是这样。而 2020 年春节前后新冠肺炎疫情蔓延，景区封闭。石林峡不怨天尤人，而是绸缪在先，趁机改造旧景。待疫情过去，石林峡再次开放，这里便全然一新了：

但见瀑布依旧，瀑下则从潭化作了一片盈盈水池。一道道随弯就势的坝阶，舒缓着瀑布的水流。池水一阶一阶地漫溢，又形成一叠一叠的瀑布。这山间白练，壁底彩池，一时间令人流连忘返。这才是：借得黄龙水一圜，更移七彩石林间！

就在瀑布飞落的瞬间，弥漫的细密水珠纷纷飘洒在身上，颇有些凉意。

细看瀑布下部，一道彩虹横挂绝壁。平时雨后天晴才有且转瞬即逝的情景，在这里只要太阳明悬峡谷上空，停住脚步，抬眼即可随时观赏了。

瀑水流过彩虹桥，顺着峡谷奔向天地间了。

Walk to the end of water and sit to watch clouds rising. The stream ends in front with cliffs and precipices on the both sides. Here is not the last scene but another stunning site in Goege Shilin. Water at the mountain top rushes out and pours straight down to the bottom in the blink of an eye. It looks like white silk hanging on a dark wall and the abrupt rocks like knives cut it into several pieces. Here is the spectacle Jiutian Waterfall (The Waterfall from the Highest of Heavens).

People usually say, despite weak power, the very unremitting efforts that you never imagine anything of will lead to the success you can never imagine. Here, the Jiutian Waterfall keeps washing the bottom stone year after year and turns it into a huge pool. Because of the wide spread of the COVID-19 pandemic in 2020, the scenic zone had to be closed temporarily. However, there is no need to blame anyone or curse the fate. The secnic zone seized the opportunity to transform the old scene and it takes an entirely brand new look now after it opens again.

Falls pouring out and down to the ground become pools of clean water. Terraced stone pools built along the landform slow the flow. Water that overflows out of the terraced pools one after another becomes continuous waterfalls below. The white-silk-like waterfall hangs on the cliff and the colorful pools at the bottom make enchanted people suspend their steps. Borrow a pool of water from dragon and you will find yourself in a colourful gorge.

九天飞瀑（摄于 2020 年 6 月）

The Jiutian Waterfall, in June 2020

At the moment when the waterfall hit the ground, its dense droplets that splash in face and body make people feel cooler.

Look closely and you can see a rainbow across over in front of the cliff. The fleeting scene that usually happens on a sunny day after rain can be seen now whenever you stop and look up.

Water flows under the rainbow and rushes forward along the gorge to the vast field.

九天飞瀑

The Jiutian Waterfall

彩虹桥

The Rainbow Bridge

飞瀑落下映射出的彩虹

The rainbow in front of the waterfall

观瀑台

The Sightseeing Platform

俯瞰九天飞瀑及七彩池（崔新民摄于 2020 年 4 月）

Overlook the The Jiutian Waterfall and the colorful pools, by Cui Xinmin in April 2020

模特装扮的七仙女下凡七彩池（摄于 2020 年 6 月 10 日直播中）

The performance of the Seven Fairies decending to the mortal world, during the web-cast on June 10, 2020)

七彩池
福

由这里往东，就是石林山顶。如果希望省时省力，游人可乘坐 700 米长的索道缆车，顺势还可俯瞰石林峡景；如果时间充裕，又有脚力，且作健身，游人也可徒步二三里山路。无论索道，还是徒步，殊途同归，都会到达山顶。

Go east to the top of the Gorge Shilin. You can take the 700-meter long sightseeing cable car to save time and energy while overlooking the landscape. If you are not in a hurry or yet exhausted, it's all right to hike two to three miles. Whatever, taking a cable car or hiking will all get you to the top.

通往石林山顶的高空索道

The cable car to the mountain top

通往石林山顶的步行路

The walkway to the mountain top

我是坐了缆车，而置身于石林峡主峰东石林山。著名的钛合金飞碟玻璃观景台，就坐落在海拔 768 米的山巅之上。当然不止这些，还有三亭及十二生肖雕像。

亭，我国园林中重要的建筑物，可以歇息，可以点景，在石林峡自然也不可或缺。这是西亭，又称钟亭，坐落在巨石之上，是一座单檐六角亭。在此，尽可观赏天地万象、四方美景。尤其园林，讲究巧于借景，“园虽别内外，得景则无拘远近”。如北京颐和园借西山之景，更显得幽深旷远。站在这里，就可观得峡谷之外的西石林山境况，更深的山间，幽静中一片人家，恍惚世外桃源。

借西石林山之景

Making use of the scenery of the West Shilin Mountain as a background

那里原有一座小山村，名叫土谷（gū）子，后来搬到山外了。

看完西石林山，再回看亭中，设有护栏。这种护栏，有个非常好听的名字，叫美人靠。坐下来，感受一下美人靠的舒服与惬意。亭里悬挂一口大铁钟，直径 1.1 米，通高 1.6 米。看看钟上镌刻的吉祥铭文，有兴致也可以敲一敲。只是别撞得了，终归是做一天和尚才撞一天钟的。

这钟应该是铸造得科学合理，以致敲起来声音洪亮、余音袅袅，满山满谷都可听到。佛教讲："闻钟声，烦恼轻。智慧长，菩提增。"在生活和工作中，也会常说或听到一个词，就是警钟长鸣。实际上，我们每每听到钟声，心灵总会受到一种震撼。

I took a cable car to the East Shilin Mountain, the main peak of Gorge Shilin. The glass sightseeing platform made of titanium alloy is constructed on the mountain top at an altitude of 768 meters; moreover, there are three pavilions and the statues of the Chinese zodiac there.

Pavilion is a typical kind of architecture in Chinese garden. People can be there for a rest as well as sightseeing. Here is the West Pavilion, also known as the Bell Pavilion. In this single-eave hexagonal pavilion located on a huge boulder, you will have a panoramic view of the gorge. The art of Chinese garden is very particular about “cleverly borrowing scenery”. The range of a garden can be divided into “the inside” and “the outside”, but the scenery of it will not be limited by distance or range. For example, the Summer Palace takes the West Mountain which is not very far behind as its background for a remote and deep sight of view. In the West Pavilion, you are able to see the further West Shilin Mountain scenery, and even the households over there.

There was a small village called Tuguzi which was then moved out of the mountain.

Turn back to the pavilion. This kind of guardrail between the pillars has a very nice name, Meiren Kao, which means “for a beautiful woman to lean on”. Why don’t you sit down and have a try. A big iron bell hanged in the middle of the pavilion is 1.6 meters in diameter and 1 meter in height. There are auspicious inscriptions engraved on the bell body. You can knock it if you want to. In Chinese, we have an old saying that so long as one remains a monk, he goes on knocking the bell, which tells us to take our responsibility.

The bell’s resonant sound trails away lingeringly all over the gorge, which must benefit from its scientific casting. Buddhism believes that the bell sound helps ease people’s inner sufferings, and the growing wisdom gets you closer to the attainment of Buddhahood. In one’s life and career, many things act as a bell that sounds the alarm for us. We usually feel deeply touched and even shocked when hearing bell sound.

西亭

The West Pavilion

西亭内大铁钟

The huge bell in the West Pavilion

西亭美人靠

The guardrails, Miren Kao, in the West Pavilion

继续沿石阶登上山顶，先看观景台北面，为十二生肖雕像，是以纯铜雕铸的站像。一般认为，十二生肖起源与原始社会氏族图腾崇拜有关，我国早在先秦之时，比较完整的生肖系统就已形成。十二生肖各有寓意，早已成为我国悠久的民俗文化符号。

这些雕像，兽首人身，整体比真人略高些。各具情态，生动传神。我属猴，一下找到属于自己的那尊，且拍照留念。

这里还有一套编钟，仿古代乐器精心制造而成。其声浑厚悠扬，是能够演奏乐曲的。我对乐曲一窍不通，随便敲上几下，实在不成曲调，赶紧作罢，让贤后面等候的人了。

Along the stone stairs, let's move forward to the mountain top. Firstly, take a look at the north of the sightseeing platform. Those exquisitely cast statues of Chinese zodiac are made of pure copper. It is generally believed that the Chinese zodiac originated with the clan totem worship in primitive society and was nearly completed in the early Qin Period. The zodiac is a long-standing cultural symbol of the Chinese folk and each of the twelve signs has its own cultural significance.

These statues with animal heads and human bodies are slightly taller than real person. Each of them looks vivid and lifelike with mien and facial expression. I was born in the year of monkey. Instantly, I found mine and took a picture with it.

There is a set of chimes which are carefully modeled on the antique musical instruments. They can be played actually and sound very melodious; however, I was born hopelessly ignorant of music and not able to make the sound in tune. I tried few times and stopped soon for those who were waiting behind me.

十二生肖雕像

The cast statues of the Chinese zodiac

龙的雕像

The statue of dragon in Chinese zodiac

仿古编钟

A set of chimes modeled on the antique musical instruments

拍完照，敲完编钟，就要走上石林山之巅，亲身体验最惊险、最刺激的钛合金飞碟玻璃观景台！观景台以航天钛金材料、合金钢、高强拉索和防弹玻璃建造而成。钛合金的重量，只有传统钢结构重量的一半，而强度则是传统钢结构的两倍。钛合金的应用，开了民间领域应用的先河。崖壁外悬空 32.8 米，面积 415 平方米，比号称世界“第八大奇景”的美国科罗拉多大峡谷廊桥还长 11 米，面积要大一倍多。

观景台以飞碟为原型，悬浮于空中，下距崖底 400 多米。玻璃晶莹剔透，下视无碍，形无所依，惊险得简直步步惊心。中间一架飞碟，里边两个外星人，一驾驶，一眺望。飞碟是刚来石林峡想降落，还是游览完石林峡要起飞呢？不得而知。

After taking pictures and sounding the chimes, we are heading to the most exciting glass sightseeing platform at the peak of the Shilin Mountain. This platform is constructed of titanium alloy, alloy steel, high strength cables and bulletproof glass. Titanium weighs half of the common steel, but it could bear twice the strength. The construction of the platform has set a precedent for the application of titanium alloy in folk sectors. It stretches out of the cliff for 32.8 meters and covers an area of 415 square meters. The platform is 11 meters longer than and twice the size of the “U” shape bridge in the American Colorado Grand Canyon which is known as the eighth wonder of the world.

The platform suspends in the air, more than 400 meters above the ground. Through the crystal and transparent glass, visitors on the platform can see clearly downwards without anything blocking the vision. The platform seems to rely on nothing and every step over there is breathtaking. There is a “spacecraft” in the middle of the platform, with two aliens inside of which one is piloting the spacecraft and the other is looking further. Maybe they are about to land or to take off. What do you think?

飞碟外星人

The ailens and their spacecraft

钛合金飞碟玻璃观景台

The glass sightseeing platform

2020 年 6 月 10 日，柴福善与北京电视台主持人燕兆麟（右）在石林峡玻璃观景台直播中

Chai Fushan and Yan Zhaolin (right) of BTV for the web-cast on the glass sightseeing platform on June 10, 2020

钛合金飞碟玻璃观景台游览盛景

The tourists on the glass sightseeing platform

NIKE
adidas

站在观景台南侧，不仅可以俯瞰雄奇险秀的石林峡全景，更可倚栏远眺，东南那片水，是山水名胜金海湖。再远些的山顶隐约可见一塔高矗，是我国历史上十五大名山之一、乾隆皇帝曾言“要知有盘山，何必下江南”的盘山。而明代万里长城从东南山间蜿蜒而来，经过黄松峪村北，继续穿山越岭向西北而去。这里为明代黄松峪关，中华人民共和国成立以后，在关口处修建一道大坝，成为黄松峪水库。

在观景台东侧，下望石林峡景区门口，有一座山乡小村雕窝村。这里有当代文学泰斗、原文化部部长王蒙的一座小院，普通的一户山里人家。曾有慕名者找到王蒙的小院，扒着门看，好奇地说：“一位享誉世界的大作家，就出自这个小院？”是，也不是。说是，因为这里确实有王蒙的家，20 多年来王蒙经常来这里读书写作，许多的小说、散文、诗歌，就是在这里写的，甚至就写的这里；说不是，因为他祖籍河北南皮，与清代张之洞为同乡，生活、工作及写作主要在京城。大家再看雕窝北面，一道山谷里坐落着另一小村塔洼，那里的村民千百年来一直在采金。

Standing on the north side of the sightseeing platform, you can not only overlook the splendid Gorge Shilin, but also look far into the distance to the mountains and the southeast water, the Jinhai Lake. A tower can be faintly seen on the peak of Panshan Mountain. The mountain is one of the most fifteen historically well-known mountains. Qing Emperor Qianlong said that if he had known the Panshan Mountain earlier, he wouldn’t have been to the south of the Yangtze River for better scenery. The Great Wall of the Ming Dynasty winding from the southeast passes by the north of the Huangsongyu Village and then crosses the mountains and ridges to the northwest. Here used to be the Huangsongyu Pass in the Ming Dynasty, and a dam was built near the pass after the founding of the People’s Republic of China. The dam has been the Huangsongyu Reservoir nowadays.

Looking downward at the entrance of Gorge Shilin Scenic Zone from the east of the sightseeing platform, you will find the small Diaowo Village. Wang Meng, the foremost master of Chinese contemporary literature and the former Minister of Culture, has lived there for more than 20 years. One of his readers once went there and squinted through the door. He couldn’t help wondering whether the world-renowned writer once really lived in this unremarkable courtyard. Actually, Wang Meng often read and wrote there before and he finished many of his novels, essays and poems, of which were about this village and his courtyard. He spent most of his time in Beijing; however, his native place is Nanpi, Hebei Province, as Zhang Zhidong's. Zhang Zhidong is a famous Qing senior officer. Tawa, another village, is at the north of Diaowo Village. People in Tawa Village from generation to generation mine gold for a living.

1999 年 5 月，王蒙（左）与柴福善在雕窝村王蒙家的核桃树下留影

Wang Meng (left) and Chai Fushan under the walnut tree in Wang's yard in the Diaowo Village in May 1999

站在观景台上向南远眺

Look into the distance to the south from the glass sightseeing platform

站在观景台上向东下眺雕窝村

Look into the distance at the Diaowo Village from the glass sightseeing platform

离开观景台，平息心境，来到石林山顶的第二座亭——中亭，这是三座亭中的主亭，位居山顶最高处，海拔 773 米。此亭为重檐六角攒尖顶，施以彩画，顶覆黄琉璃瓦。

彩画大致分为三种，和玺彩画，等级最高，主要是画以龙或凤图案，沥粉贴金，辉煌壮丽。和玺彩画主要用于紫禁城外朝重要建筑及内廷中帝后居住的等级较高的宫殿等。旋子彩画，等级次于和玺彩画，主要画以简化形式的涡卷瓣旋花，有时也画龙凤，一般用于次要宫殿或寺庙中。苏式彩画，等级低于前两种。主要画以山水、人物故事、花鸟鱼虫等。一般用于园林中的小型建筑，如亭、台、廊、榭以及四合院住宅、垂花门的额枋上。这么看来，这亭上的彩画当属于苏式彩画了。

我是坐在美人靠上略作休息，并顺便欣赏了一下彩画的。

在绝顶北眺，才发现绝顶并非极顶，峰峰岭岭连绵起伏涌向天际，正是莽莽苍苍的燕山！

Stay in detachment and let's move on. Here we are at the second pavilion——the Middle Pavilion, which is the main one among the three pavilions here. The Middle Pavilion at the peak of the mountain is 773 meters above sea level. The double-eave hexagonal pavilion with a spire is exquisitedly painted and roofed with golden glazed tile.

Paintings on Chinese traditional buildings could be generally divided into three types: Hexi painting, the highest level of these three types, is mostly applied to the important buildings at the south of the Gate of Heavenly Purity and the palaces of higher hierarchy for emperors and empresses at the north of the Gate of Heavenly Purity in the Forbidden City. These buildings and palaces are usually painted with dragon and phoenix patterns and decorated with gold foil. Then, Xuanzi painting is characterized by simplified duplicated scroll patterns, sometimes with dragon and phoenix patterns, and is generally used in the secondary palaces and temples. Inferior to the first two types, Sushi painting is usually about landscape, characters and their stories, flowers and animals like birds, fish and insects. It is mostly applied to small buildings like pavilions, terraces, corridors in gardens and the overhead

站在中亭向北眺望莽莽燕山

Look into the distance at the Yanshan Mountains in the Middle Pavilion beams of quadrangles and gates. Accordingly, the paintings on the Middle Pavilion are Shushi paintings.

I appreciated these paintings in passing while having a break leaning against the railing.

Gazing north from the hilltop, I figured that the hilltop under my feet was not the extremely high site. Peak after peak, ridge by ridge, mountains undulate and extend to the further sky where is the Yanshan Hills.

中亭

The Middle Pavilion

中亭内彩画之一

One of the Sushi paintings on the Middle Pavilion

中亭内彩画之二

One of the Sushi paintings on the Middle Pavilion

这是石林山顶的第三座亭——东亭，亦称鼓亭，也是一座单檐六角亭，比主亭略小些。亭中置一铜鼓，重达 800 斤，击鼓声震天地。

古人常以击鼓为进，在战场上，就是击鼓进兵，而鸣金收兵。常说的一个词，就是一鼓作气。一击鼓，总会长人精神，使人振奋。

那是谁，兴趣盎然，击了一通又一通鼓。

Here is the third pavilion on the Shilin hilltop——the East Pavilion, also known as the Drum Pavilion. The single-eave hexagonal pavilion is slightly smaller than the Middle Pavilion. A bronze drum of 400kg in weight is hanged in the middle of the pavilion and sounds ear-splitting.

On the ancient battlefields, people signaled with drums to advance and with Zheng, a bronze-made instrument, to withdraw. We always encourage people to "press on to the finish without letup", a Chinese idiom which originated from a story in the Spring and Autumn Period of the ancient China. It is about effectively stimulating the army morale by beating drums at an opportune moment. Rhythmed Drumbeats always make people heartened and encouraged.

Look! Who is there having fun at beating the drum over and over again?

铜鼓

The copper drum in the East Pavilion

东亭

The East Pavilion

从这里要下山了，有一段石阶路，还有栈道，又曲折，又陡峭。想想，世间的路哪能都平坦呢？前面可以坐缆车，也可以走步道，都可以到走进石林峡时的柿树林那里。

石林峡栈道，多倚着崖壁修建，随高就低，随弯就直，随里就外，随上就下，既为峡谷之路，又是景区一景。像刚才走上石林峡主亭中亭时，登着几个“脚印”，沿着西侧巨石而上。这脚印形状的铁制的踏步，当是一种特殊的栈道了。

栈道，原指沿悬崖峭壁凿孔架构的一种道路。历史上，最为人们熟知的一个故事是：秦末楚汉相争，项羽封刘邦为汉王，刘邦势弱，用张良之计，烧毁几百里栈道，以示再无回关中之心，使项羽疏于戒备。而后，有人起兵反项。刘邦再依韩信之计，明修栈道，暗度陈仓，乘机攻占关中，为建立大汉王朝奠定基础。

It is time to go down. There will be a section of stone steps and walkways that are not very flat or straight ahead. You can go down by cable car or by foot and finally reach the persimmon trees which you have passed by when you went into Gorge Shilin.

Usually built against sheer precipices, trestle roads here follow the landform of the mountains and make use of their natural terrains. These roads are scenery themselves. Just now, we stepped on the iron “footprints” along the west boulders to the Middle Pavilion. Those footprint-shaped iron steps organize a special trestle road.

When it comes to trestle road, it usually refers to the plank roads built on wooden brackets fixed into cliffs. The most well-known story about trestle road happened during the war between two hostile regimes Chu and Han at the end of the Qin Dynasty. Xiang Yu, the king of Chu, bestowed the title of the feudatory King of Han on Liu Bang. To show his loyalty to Xiang Yu, Liu Bang who was in an unfavorable situation accepted others’ suggestion to burn up the hundreds of miles of plank roads leading to the territories that were under Xiang’s control. It meant he would never cross the border nor enter Xiang’s territories. Actions taken by Liu Bang slacken Xiang Yu’s vigilance. Then, some people rose up against Xiang Yu, and Liu Bang seized the opportunity to repair plank roads while making a secret detour. He finally took the region of Guanzhong, which laid the foundation for the establishment of the Han Dynasty.

石林峡栈道

The trestle roads in Gorge Shilin

中亭巨石西侧脚印状的铁制踏步和栈道

The stepping stairs in the shape of footprints and the trestle roads on the west of the Middle Pavilion

石林峡栈道

The trestle roads in Gorge Shilin

石林峡景区门外北侧，有萌宠观光互动区，松鼠、兔子、羊驼、矮马、孔雀、火鸡等一批大小动物，极其可爱。有大人带孩子参观及饲喂互动，享受着无尽的欢乐。

On the north side of the scenic zone entrance, there is a mini zoo with animals like squirrel, rabbit, alpaca, pony, peacock and turkey in it. Kids accompained by their parents can feed and pet those lovely friends with great joy.

保驾宝宝骑矮马

Protect the kids during horseback riding

温顺的羊驼

Mild alpacas

北京电视台主持人石雨濛与小朋友一起喂羊驼（摄于 2020 年 6 月 10 日直播中）

Kids and Shi Yumeng of BTV feeding alpaca, during the web-cast on June 10, 2020

孩子与小白兔

The kids and rabbits

石林峡景区门外南侧，还有高空飞翔、自悬滑车等惊险、刺激的游乐项目。当然也有旋转木马、碰碰车、旋转恐龙等，既可亲子互动，又可让年长者追忆逝去的童年。

In the amusement park on the south side of the entrance, people can have fun at the exciting projects like "Flying High" or "Self-suspending Car"; moreover, there are facilities for kids such as carousels, bumper cars and spinning dinosaur. Parents can join in together and these activities could help the grown up recall their childhoods.

鲨鱼岛

The Shark-Island

旋转木马

Carousels

高空飞翔

Flying High

景区门前广场，有一重点推出的黄金文化观赏体验项目。

平谷盛产黄金，北部连绵群山，因此称为大金山。而平谷关于黄金的历史，起码可追溯到商代中期，南独乐河镇刘家河发现的商代中期墓葬，专家研究认为是座方国领袖墓。至于是什么方国，目前没有定论。墓中出土随葬器物40余件，其中青铜礼器16件，具有商代风格和特征，墓中还出土种类较多且器形较大的金器，有金臂钏2件，金耳环和金笄（jī，古代束发的簪子）各1件。金笄长达27.7厘米，重达108.7克。这就把平谷地区使用黄金的历史提早到商代中期，约3300年前。平谷黄金开采一般认为始于唐代，延续至今。中华人民共和国成立后，建国营金矿，最高产量曾达一万余两，故平谷称黄金万两县。后来又有民采。随着社会发展，尤其近年重视生态环境保护，已关闭金矿，禁止私挖乱采了。

In the front plaza is the thematic showcase of the gold culture.

The northern continuous mountains are Dajin Mountains. Pinggu District abounds with gold, and its history related to it can be traced back to the mid-Shang Dynasty. Here is the tomb of the mid-Shang Dynasty discovered at Liujiahe, South Dule Town. It was deduced that the tomb belonged to the leader of a southern state, but no one knows for sure which state it was. More than 40 funeral objects buried with the dead had been unearthed, including 16 bronze ritual vessels which reflected the style and characteristics of Shang Dynasty and many types of larger golden utensils, such as two armlets, one earring and one hairpin which is called "jī" in Chinese and written as " 笄 ". This hairpin is 108.7g heavy and 27.7cm long, which proves that the use of gold in Pinggu District can be traced back to the mid-Shang Dynasty, nearly 3300 B.C.. The gold mining in Pinggu District is generally believed to have started in Tang Dynasty and lasts until now. After the founding of the People's Republic of China, gold mines here became state-owned and the highest output reached more than 10,000 tales gold, which won the reputation for Pinggu. Then, private mining was allowed as well. However, the government gradually closed the gold fields and then fully prohibited unauthorized mining, as the environmental protection became more and more important for the needs of social development.

平谷区南独乐河镇刘家河商墓出土器物之金臂钏

The golden armlets unearthed in Liujiahe, South Dule Town, Pinggu District

20 世纪 80 年代末 90 年代初，平谷过去的土法淘金

The traditional way of panning in Pinggu District, in the late 1980s and early 1990s

平谷区南独乐河镇刘家河商墓出土器物之三羊铜罍

The golden wine-vessel unearthed in Liujiahe, South Dule Town, Pinggu District

平谷区南独乐河镇刘家河商墓出土器物之金笄

The golden hairpin unearthed in Liujiahe, South Dule Town, Pinggu District

平谷地区有不少关于黄金的传说。比如北边不远有座牛金坨，老辈人传说：过去有人到这里放牛，10 头牛到这儿就多 1 头，变成 11 头了，每天如此。放牛人有心，在多出的牛身上做个记号。等那头牛想钻进山里时，放牛的人赶紧往外拽，一下拽掉了牛尾巴。回来一看，牛尾巴是金子的，这山岭就叫牛金坨了。还有金牛拉着金碾子、轧金豆子等传说。这些传说，应该与北部山区向来产金有关。

There are many legends about gold in Pinggu District. Not very far to the north is a ridge called Niujintuo. The old folks say that people in the past usually herded cattle there before. If you took 10 cows, you would have brought 11 cows back, which happened every time you herded cattle. Then, a cattleman purposely marked the extra cow and grabbed it by the tail tightly when it tended to go back to the mountain, and pulled off its tail. When he went back home, the cattleman found the tail had turned into a piece of gold. That's how this ridge got its name, Niujintuo; moreover, there are other legends like a golden cow becoming a millstone and making golden beans. The origin of all these legends should be related to its long history of gold mining and production in the northern mountainous regions.

平谷区镇罗营镇见子庄村东北牛金坨
（摄于 2014 年 12 月）

Niujintuo, a ridge on the northeast
Jianzizhuang Village, Zhenluoying Town,
Pinggu District, in December 2014

为展示黄金文化，石林峡景区在挖掘当地黄金文化的基础上，融入传统民俗祥瑞寓意，斥巨资以纯金精心打造了龙凤金娃、净手金盆以及金勺、金壶、金盏等 10 多件艺术珍品。共用黄金 93 斤，其中男娃 22 斤，女娃 21 斤，佩戴和田白玉，点缀南红玛瑙，富丽堂皇，活泼可爱。应该说，这是继钛合金飞碟玻璃观景台之后，石林峡景区重点打造的又一全新项目，很值得亲身体验。

To widely show and spread the culture of gold, the gold mining and the traditional folk and auspicious culture have been intently integrated. Ten more artworks made of solid gold such as boy and girl dolls, hand-cleaning basin, spoon, pot and cups have been exquisitely made, which costs 46.5kg of gold. Among them, the golden boy doll weights 11kg and the girl doll 10.5kg. Decorated with Hetian Jade and red agate, they look pretty and lovely. Besides the glass sightseeing platform, the gold culture showcase is another brand new project for visitors and it is totally worth your time.

石林峡金娃体验馆

The gold culture showcase zone

金娃体验馆
石林峡
免费参观
迎福金娃
拍照体验

龙凤金娃

The golden boy and girl dolls

著名网红尧十六在石林峡抱金娃娃

Yao Shiliu, an online celebrity with a golden doll in her arms

净手金盆及金勺

The golden hand-cleaning basin and spoon

金壶、金盏

The golden pot and cups

这大半日，行走在这一派明净的山水中，与这山、与这水、与这天地，相悠游、相偎依、相守望。就在与自然的交接中，我的心境舒展，精神更健旺了。

石林峡景，终与云南石林不同。常说十里不同俗，百里不同天，何况一在清新秀美的南方，一在雄浑豪放的北方，应该各有千秋的。

During the visit of more than half of a day, I felt fully integrated with nature. The isolated world of green mountains and clean water here refreshed my mind and brought me inner peace.

Compared with the gorges in Yunnan Province, Gorge Shilin looks definitely distinctive. It is often said that countrysides which are ten miles far away from each other have different traditions, and regions hundreds miles away from each other boast distinctive landscape, not to mention the gorges in the elegant south and in the magnificent north of China.

云南石林

The gorges in Yunnan Province

石林峡的山

The mountains in Gorge Shilin

石林峡的水

The water in Gorge Shilin

石林峡的石与桥

The rocks and bridges in Gorge Shilin

后记

一场突如其来的疫情，一下改变了人们出行的习惯，也极大地催生和发展了旅游直播。因我多年研究家乡历史文化，对平谷山水人文有些了解，也就顺其自然地客串起了直播人。先是五月丫髻山直播，而后是六月石林峡直播。待播完下山，直播者告诉我，每次观众都达 100 多万！直播影响之大，超乎我的想象。

应该说，对石林峡我是熟悉的。这些年来，我自己或陪客人多次游览，峡谷的一山一水一草一木都使我流连忘返，兴之所至还随手写了些文字。发表于《北京日报》的《石林峡览胜》，一步一景地全面呈现了石林峡，后来制作成风光片，请赵忠祥先生朗诵。发表于《人民日报》的《再访石林峡》，是在疫情得到基本控制、景区新增项目之后，我再次游览所记。

尽管我对石林峡有一定了解，但面对镜头直播，一路上我应该从哪里解说，解说到什么程度，感觉以前的积累似乎远远不够。于是，我又几番上山，且仔细收集资料，悉心酝酿，着手编写，经十几次修改补充完善，最终完成这篇《畅游石林峡》文本。文本基本依照游览线路，描写诸多景观，融汇相关文化知识，以及我对社会、对人生的一些感悟。通过我之口，让人们更好地认识石林峡，并在石林峡和游客之间建立情感上的联结，以便游客前来游览时，能够全身心享受这山明水净的大自然。

文友柳小军看后，认为这是以艺术之笔，把自然山水与人文精神相融合，混沌一体，赋予了石林峡历史之韵、文化之气、山水之魂，这本身就是一道美丽的风景。他略加整理，就做了书前卷首语。景区负责人也说，所写的就是石林峡，打算把文本制作成说明标牌，放置在景观前，以导人游览。

我由此萌生编制一本导游册的念头，让人一册在手，尽览石林峡风光。为此，选择天晴日，从文本表述的视角，重新拍摄石林峡每一处景观，并找出以前拍摄的一些旧照，石林峡亦提供了部分照片资料，使之成为一本图文并茂的手边书。

我自知才疏学浅，尤其对于摄影更是门外汉，没多高艺术价值可言，只求写实写真，具体表现了文本内容而已。因此，书中有这样那样的不足，实在所难免，敬请方家同人及读者不吝赐教。

柴福善

2020 年 6 月 24 日于善书斋

Postscript

The sudden befalling COVID-19 pandemic changed our ways to travel and greatly promoted tourism web-cast. I spent years on the history and culture of Pinggu District, my hometown, and I have learned lots about its natural attractions and humanistic culture. So I naturally joined in the web-cast in Yaji Mountain in May and then in Gorge Shilin in July. To my surprise, more than one million audiences watched the web-casts every time.

Over the years, I have visited Gorge Shilin many times by myself or with others. I am familiar with it. Its mountains and rivers, blossoms and trees make me linger every time. Sometimes I felt really in the mood to write pieces of words to remember those bright things. My work *The Spotlights in Gorge Shilin*, published in Beijing Daily, elaborately introduced the scenic zone, and was adopted into a scenic film dubbed by Zhao Zhongxiang, a well known host of CCTV. Some brand new showcases and spotlights were added, so I visit here again and wrote *To Be There in Gorge Shilin One More Time* which was published in People's Daily then.

I thought I certainly knew enough about Gorge Shilin. However, during the web-casts, I had no idea where to start or how much I should talk. I haven't learn enough about it before. So I went up there more times and elaborately accumulated information. After a dozen times of revision, addition and improvement, *The Rock Wonderland——Gorge Shilin* has been finally done. Basically following the visit route, it involves many spotlights and integrates relevant cultural knowledge and my perceptions about life. All I have tried is to help people know more about Gorge Shilin, and maybe establish an emotional connection to enjoy the great nature of bright mountains and clean water.

After reading this, my friend Liu Xiaojun wrote in the preface that it introduces Gorge Shilin's history and culture and shows the charm of its mountains and water. Its natural landscape and humanistic value are merged into a unity. As I knew, the manager of this scenic zone intended to adopt my writings to make introduction signs for tourists.

The idea to compile a tourist guide book came to me one day. I hope it can do some help for every visitor to enjoy their time in Gorge Shilin. For this, I took pictures again for every beauty spot here on a sunny day. With pictures taken before and some materials provided by the scenic zone, this book will be illustrated.

I know I am not talented, and quite new in photographing, so what I am trying to do is to show how Gorge Shilin is really like. Undoubtedly, there will be much can be improved in this book and I am open to advice from the professional and readers.

Chai Fushan

At Shanshu Study, June 24, 2020

策　　划：彭明榜
责任编辑：王佳慧　胡一鸣
责任印制：谢　雨
书籍设计：孙　初　文小婧

图书在版编目（CIP）数据

畅游石林峡：汉英对照 / 柴福善著 . -- 北京：中国旅游出版社，2020.12
ISBN 978-7-5032-5602-8

Ⅰ . ①畅… Ⅱ . ①柴… Ⅲ . ①旅游指南－平谷区－汉、英 Ⅳ . ① K928.913

中国版本图书馆 CIP 数据核字 (2020) 第 219925 号

书　　名：畅游石林峡

作　　者：柴福善　著
出版发行：中国旅游出版社
(北京静安东里 6 号　邮编：100028)
http://www.cttp.net.cn　E-mail:cttp@mct.gov.cn
营销中心电话：010-57377108，010-57377109
读者服务部电话：010-57377151
排　　版：北京小众雅集文化传媒有限公司
印　　刷：北京精彩世纪印刷科技有限公司
版　　次：2020 年 12 月第 1 版　2020 年 12 月第 1 次印刷
开　　本：889 毫米 ×1194 毫米　1/16
印　　张：8.25
字　　数：88 千
定　　价：98.00 元
I S B N　978-7-5032-5602-8